All About

FLAGS

Awesome Activity Book

Fun Facts, Mazes, Games, and Brain Teasers

Edited by
Paola Misesti

Illustrations by
Agnese Baruzzi

FLAGS
A World Just Waiting
to Be Discovered!

Geography is a fascinating subject for children and adults alike, allowing you to discover the world we live in. This book is all about **VEXILLOLOGY**, or the study of flags, a subject that captures our curiosity, no matter our age.

This story is about two young apprentices, Gea and Tom, and a flag expert, Ben, who'll help the children learn the secrets and principles behind designing a flag. They'll discover the characteristics and peculiarities of flags, find out what they're used for, explore some in detail, and by the end of the book, Gea and Tom will know how to design one.

Following the principles outlined by NAVA (the North American Vexillological Association), your child will learn all about the different types of flags and their purposes. They'll analyze the principles of flag design and learn the mistakes to avoid. These rules will be explored throughout the book, and their importance will be explained. Readers will be given the opportunity to put their acquired knowledge into practice by designing their own flags.

At the end of the story, each reader will be awarded an apprentice vexillologist's rosette.

While all of the activities are presented in the form of fun and practical games, they also provide loads of information and fun facts about the world of flags.

A few notes about the activities

The order of the activities is designed to allow children to acquire knowledge gradually and easily, and we recommend following the story page by page.

There's a mix of simple and complex activities, making the book engaging and stimulating for children of different ages. You'll also find materials to cut out for making crafts, each accompanied by detailed and illustrated explanations. All of the activities are designed for children to do on their own, but adult supervision and interaction is always best, especially for younger children. There are also eight pages of stickers to use within the book and a section at the end with all the answers to the activities.

The Future Geographers Club

Hi!

My name's Gea, and I'm an aspiring geographer. I love geography and anything related to studying the earth. I'd like to introduce you to two friends of mine: Tom, who wants to be a cartographer, and Ben, who's crazy about flags and knows absolutely everything about designing them. We all belong to the "**Future Geographers Club**." If you'd like to know more about us, take a look at our membership cards.

The Future Geographers Club

FIRST NAME: Gea
LAST NAME: Welt
AGE: 10
HOBBIES: Geography, reading, photography, minerals
FAVORITE ANIMAL: Panda
FAVORITE COLOR: Purple

The Future Geographers Club

FIRST NAME: Tom
LAST NAME: Compass
AGE: 11
HOBBIES: Cartography, video games
FAVORITE ANIMAL: Chameleon
FAVORITE COLOR: Green

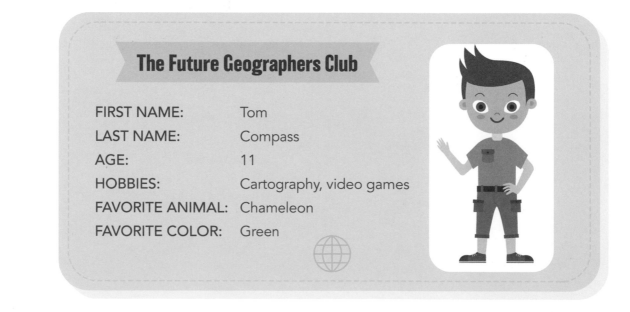

The Future Geographers Club

FIRST NAME: Ben

LAST NAME: Flaggy

AGE: 11

HOBBIES: Vexillology, photography, science fiction

FAVORITE ANIMAL: Tiger

FAVORITE COLOR: Orange

Welcome to the Club!

You can join the Future Geographers Club, too!
Fill out the membership card below, then
attach a photo or drawing of yourself!

The Future Geographers Club

FIRST NAME: _____

LAST NAME: _____

AGE: _____

HOBBIES: _____

_____

FAVORITE ANIMAL: _____

FAVORITE COLOR: _____

A Multitude of Flags!

Do you know why I like flags so much? Because they're everywhere and are used for lots of different purposes.

Put an X in the box next to the flags you recognize, and then write where you saw them. Now connect them to the people who use them, using the stickers at the back of the book. But beware: there are some stickers you won't use!

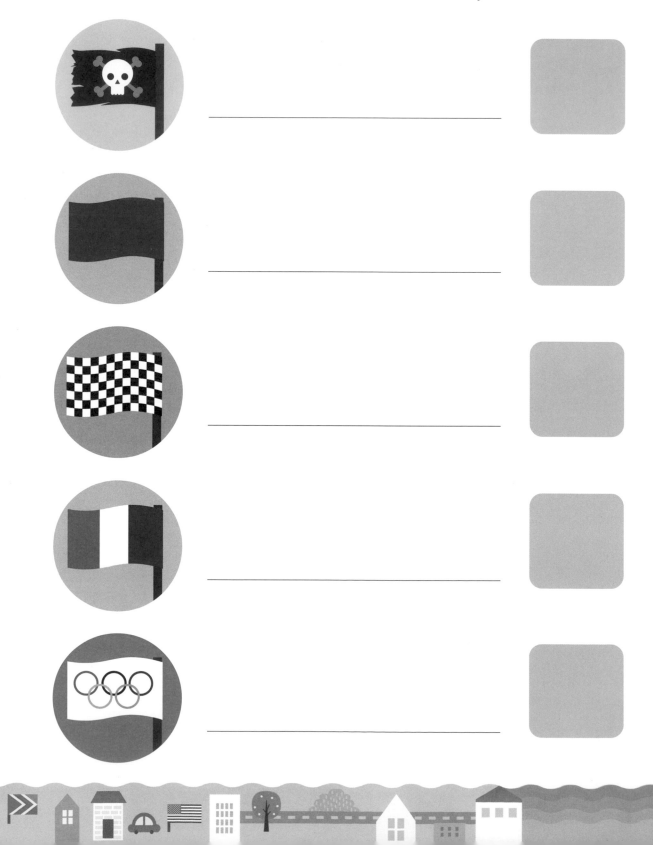

Let's Study Flags

Do you know what the study of flags is called?

Some of the flags below have numbers next to them. Match each number with a numbered space below. Then write the first letter of the flag's country in the space.

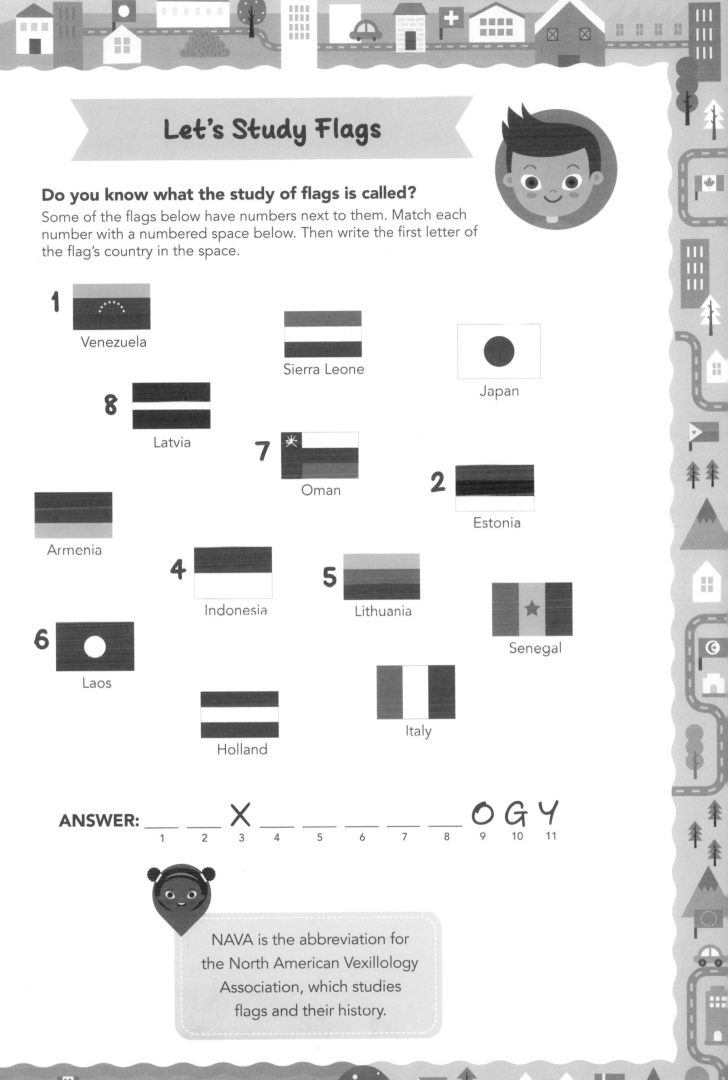

1 Venezuela

Sierra Leone

Japan

8 Latvia

7 Oman

Armenia

2 Estonia

4 Indonesia

5 Lithuania

Senegal

6 Laos

Holland

Italy

ANSWER: ___ ___ X ___ ___ ___ ___ ___ O G Y
        1   2   3   4   5   6   7   8   9 10 11

NAVA is the abbreviation for the North American Vexillology Association, which studies flags and their history.

What Are Flags Used For?

Flags are used to identify a place, an organization, or a person. They can also be used for signaling.

Flags are designed to be seen from a **distance** and can be reproduced in various sizes. Connect the flags below with how they are used by writing the correct number on the line next to the picture. Warning: There are two uses listed below that you won't need!

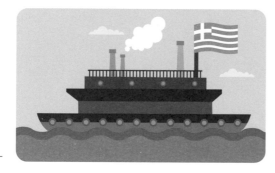

1 • **Represents a game**

2 • **Represents the symbol of an event**

3 • **Identifies a group of people**

4 • **Indicates the owner of a property**

5 • **Indicates the color of a dress**

6 • **Indicates the nationality of a ship**

Just Flags?

Do you know what the difference between a flag and a banner is?

A **banner** is a piece of embroidered or painted cloth attached to a pole. Banners aren't flown. They are meant to be seen close up, and the design is only on one side. They're used to represent groups of people, religious groups, or communal groups.

A **flag** identifies a place, an organization, or a person. They are also used for signaling.

Find and circle the **flags** among the banners below.

A Little Bit of History

In ancient times, flags were used for military purposes, to identify armies or ships.

They were later used to represent kingdoms, empires, countries, organizations, companies, sports teams, and political parties. Using what you learned in the previous activities to help you, find the **right flag stickers** to complete the pictures.

The Oldest Flag in the World

Flags appeared thousands of years ago.
Archaeologists think that the oldest flag in the world was made with bronze and is about 5,000 years old! Try completing it with the stickers.

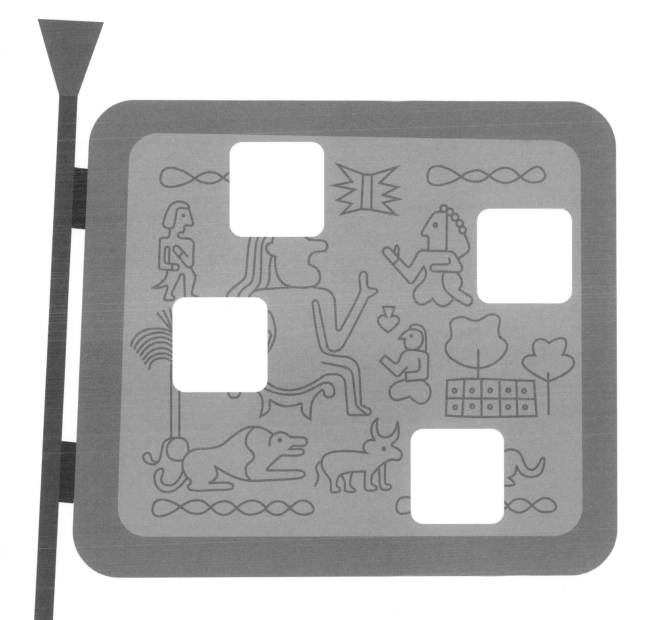

What Is a Flag Composed Of?

This is what a flag is composed of.

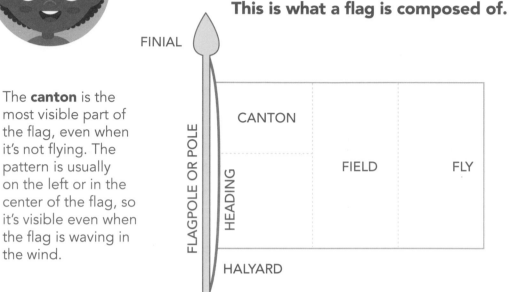

FINIAL

FLAGPOLE OR POLE

CANTON

HEADING

FIELD

FLY

HALYARD

The **canton** is the most visible part of the flag, even when it's not flying. The pattern is usually on the left or in the center of the flag, so it's visible even when the flag is waving in the wind.

In the flags below, circle:
• the canton in **orange**
• the fly in **blue**
• the field of the flag in **black**

Did you notice where the symbol is?

Samoan Islands

China

Brazil

Togo

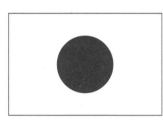
Japan

Liechtenstein

So Many Shapes!

National flags are usually rectangular because they fly better.

You can find national flags in other shapes, though, too! For example, the Swiss flag is a square. Did you know that the flag of **Nepal** is the only one in the world that is neither rectangular nor square?

Nepal

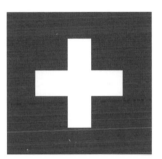
Switzerland

Help Tom find the **non-rectangular flag** among those below.

India

Seychelles

Spain

Panama

Mexico

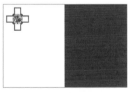
Malta

Vatican City

Pakistan

Grenada

A Flag Design Manual

NAVA has written a book that explains the five principles for designing an exceptional flag.

To find out what the **five principles** are, think about the flags you know and answer the questions below. If you write the correct answer letters in the matching numbered spaces below, you'll discover my favorite animal!

5

A **GOOD** flag must be:
- the same as another one   A
- small   O
- different from all the others   R

3

You **have** to use:
- a few colors   G
- 20 or more colors   T
- yellow   R

1

A **GOOD** flag must be:
- round   F
- simple   T
- made up of circles   A

4

You **mustn't** use:
- blue   U
- fabric   S
- lettering   E

2

A **GOOD** flag must have:
- meaningful symbols   I
- lots of triangles   G
- a hole   A

ANSWER: ____ ____ ____ ____ ____
             1   2   3   4   5

Simplicity

Do you know what the first principle to making a good flag is? Simplicity.

Flags have to be simple so that they are
• recognizable at a **distance**
• easy to **remember** and draw
• always **distinguishable**, even when they are small or printed in black and white

Look at these two flags: which one do you think is easier to draw?

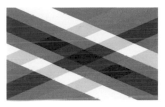

Now it's your turn!
Copy these two flags, then indicate which one you think is simpler, and therefore a good flag!

 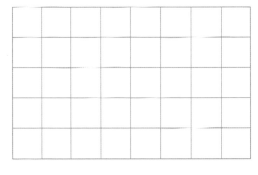

_____

 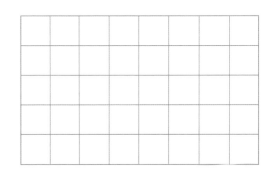

_____

A Matter of Distance

A good flag must also be recognizable from a distance.
Look carefully at the two pictures below, and then help Gea
find the matching flags among those on the right.
Which one did you match the quickest?

A Memory Game

A good flag must be easy to remember.

I challenged Tom to a fun memory game. Let's play it together!
Look at these three flags for a minute, then cover them and try to draw them in the box on the right.
When you've finished, see if you got it right.
Which of your three drawings is the closest to the original?

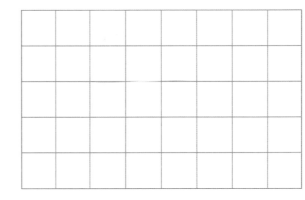

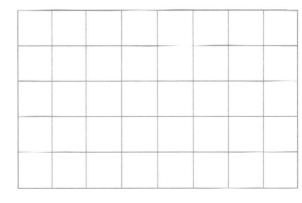

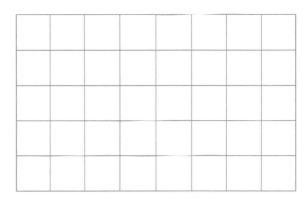

Simpler flags are easier to remember and easier to draw!

Black and White

Sometimes flags have to be reproduced in black and white.

Tom has to find the colored stickers that match these black and white flags. Can you help him? Be careful not to get confused; some of them look alike!

That was fun! I recognized the simpler flags more quickly!

When we design a flag, it's best not to use lettering or words.

You wouldn't be able to read them from a distance, they are difficult to reproduce on fabric, and they would have to be written on both the front and the back to be legible.

Look at my flag! What would happen if we wrote my name on only one side?

We'd see my name written backward on the back! What can we use to make it clear that this is my flag? That's right: **symbols**! For example, if someone likes volleyball and the color purple, their flag could look like this:

Now it's your turn: you can either use the symbols below or use one of your own. Design your flag, using your favorite color and one of your hobbies.

To make a flag that's simple and easy to recognize and draw, it's best to use just one symbol.

Hidden Meanings

Flags can have many meanings. These are expressed by how the colors are arranged and the symbols on them. Here are some examples:

The colors in the **Ukrainian** flag represent **wheat fields** and the **sky**.

The blue in the **Micronesian** flag represents the **ocean**, and the four stars represent the **island groups** in the federation.

The **maple leaf** on the **Canadian** flag represents the country's national tree.

Now it's your turn! I designed some flags with symbols of things I love.
Match the flags with the things they symbolize, using the **stickers** at the back of the book.

Beastly Flags

Some countries' flags depict stylized animals.

Find the stickers of the animals below, and attach them next to the description of the flag.

On the flag of **Wyoming**, a state of the United States of America, there is a **bison**, which once roamed the immense prairies in the Wild West. Today, the bison is almost extinct … but not on the flag!

The **Sri Lankan** flag is dominated by a **lion**. You might think this is because lions live there, but you'd be wrong! It's actually the symbol of one of the country's ethnic groups.

The **Ugandan** flag depicts a bird: a **crested crane**, which is the country's national symbol.

On the flag of **Papua New Guinea**, there is a **bird of paradise**, the country's national symbol.

A Flag Alphabet!

Do you know what the International Maritime Signal Flags are?

They're flags that stand for letters and numbers. Ships use them to communicate.

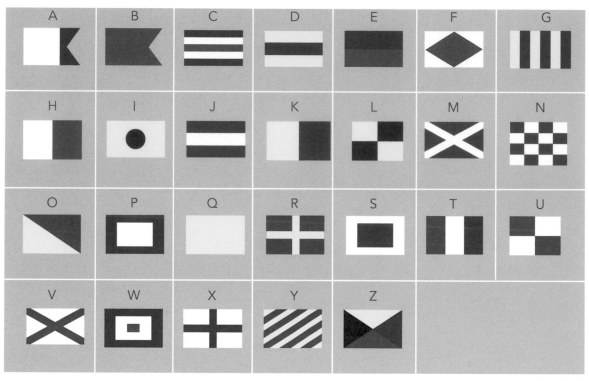

Use the stickers to try and write our names with the flags.
Now, try writing your name in flags on a piece of paper!

TOM

BEN

GEA

The following international maritime signal flags represent numbers.

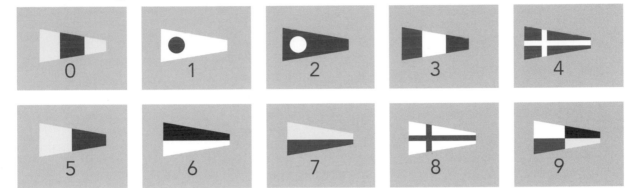

0   1   2   3   4

5   6   7   8   9

Shall we try using flags to answer these math questions? Use the stickers to indicate the answers, as shown in the example.

10 + 6 = 16

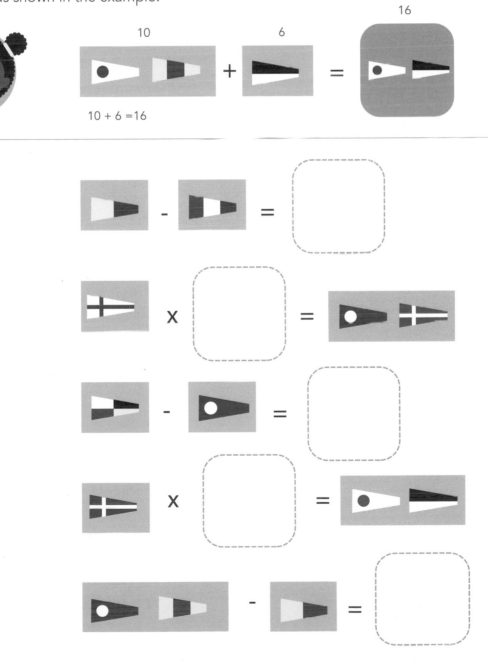

Guess the Flag!

The object of this game is to guess which flag the other player has.

1. It's a game for two players. Prepare the playing cards: attach the stickers at the back of the book to a piece of cardboard, then cut them out.

2. Each player draws a card from the deck, without showing it to their opponent: this is the flag that the other player has to guess. Whoever guesses first, wins.

3. Get a large book and stand it up between the two pages of this book, close to the spine, so that neither player can see the other's flag. Each player will have one of the two game boards.

PLAYER 1

4. Each player must get 20 small objects to cover eliminated flags.

5. The first player asks a question, for example: "Does your flag have two colors?" Depending on the answer, they will cover the flags that do not match the description.

6. The players take turns asking questions to eliminate flags. The winner is the one who guesses their opponent's flag first!

PLAYER 2

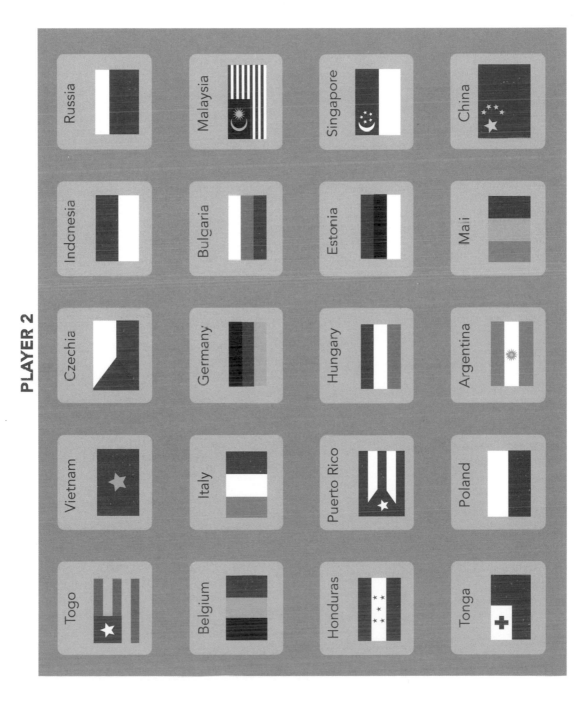

How Many Colors?

It's easier to recognize our flags if we use a maximum of four colors.
They are also easier to identify from a distance.
In both of the pictures below, the flags on the buildings have just one **small difference**.
What is it?

In which picture is the difference easier to spot?

 Now look closely at the flag below, then find the differences in those on the right. There is a **small difference** on all except one. Which flag is the same as the original?

 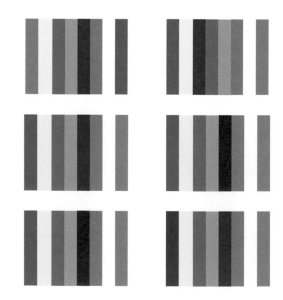

The colors used in national flags can have meanings. For example: Red can represent strength, white can represent peace, and blue can represent the sky or water.

The Color Die

Gea and I made up a really fun game.

Cut the **die** out and then fold all the sides inward.
Put glue on the gray tabs, where "glue" is written on them, and stick all the sides together. Now, turn the page and come and play with us!

glue

glue

glue

glue

glue

glue

This is what your color die should look like!

All Different!

Let's see if it's possible to create 20 different flags by only using the colors on the die.

For each flag, roll the die 3 times, then color it according to the colors you roll. But be careful: all the flags must be different, and none should be only one color.

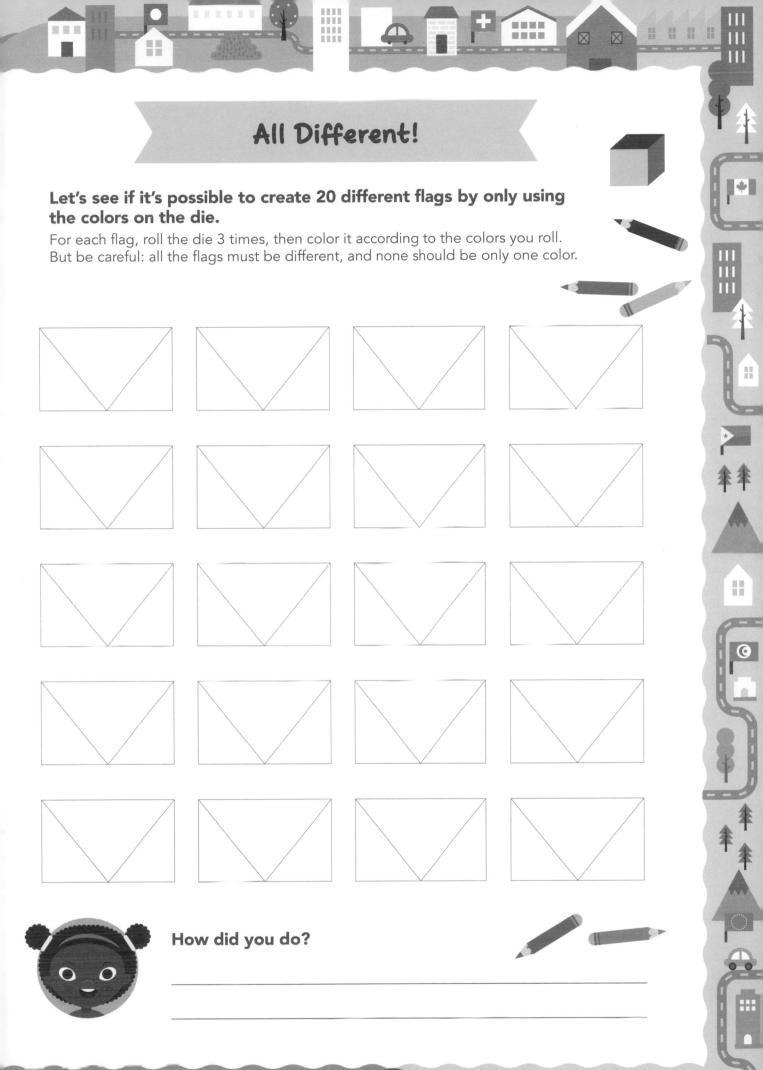

How did you do?

_____

_____

A Matter of Contrast

Ben told us a secret!

To design a good flag, it's best to use **different and contrasting colors**, alternating a light color with a dark one. This way the colors stand out better and the flags are easier to recognize from a distance!

Flag with contrasting colors

Flag with similar colors

Look at these flags.
Some of them **lack color contrast**. Circle these, then find similar flags with **more contrasting colors** among the stickers and stick them on top!

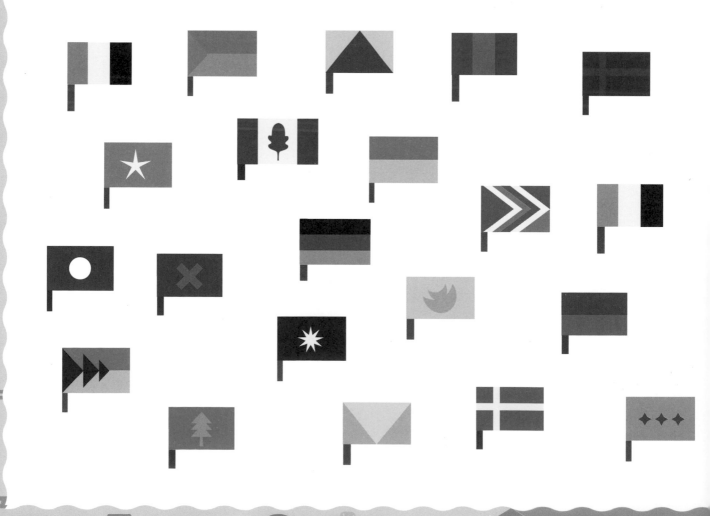

Get Out of the Maze

Designing a flag with the right colors and sequence is very important, and Ben knows it.

Help him reach Gea by following the path of **good flags** through the **maze**.
The flags with low color contrast will lead him to dead ends!

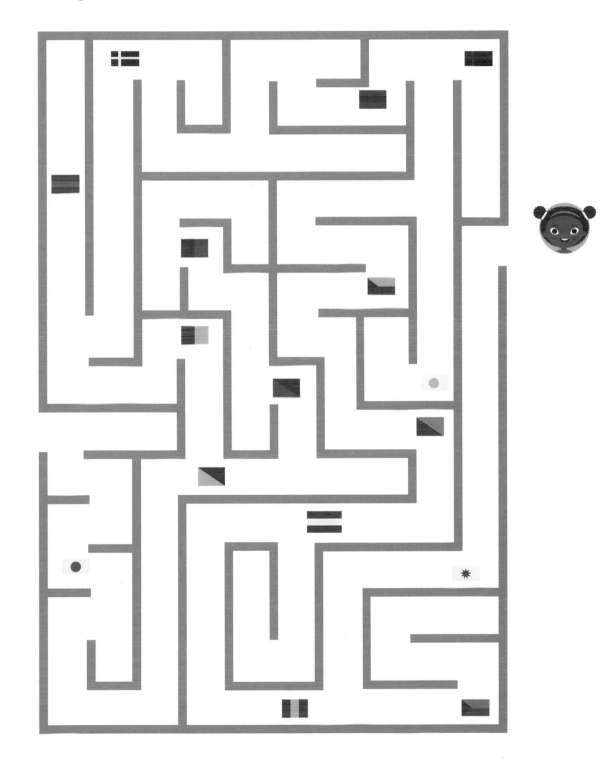

The Symmetry Game

Some flags are symmetrical: if you fold them in half, the two sides overlap perfectly.

Canada

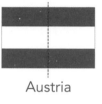
Austria

Poland

Switzerland

Help Tom **reproduce** some flags by drawing and coloring the missing part.
Remember, it has to be exactly the same as the other side. Use the dotted lines to help you!

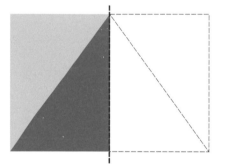

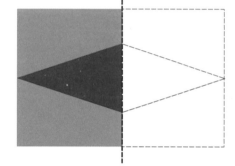

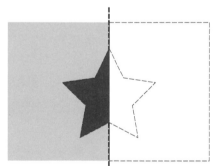

Harder and **harder**!
Now, complete the flags yourself, without the help of any dotted lines!

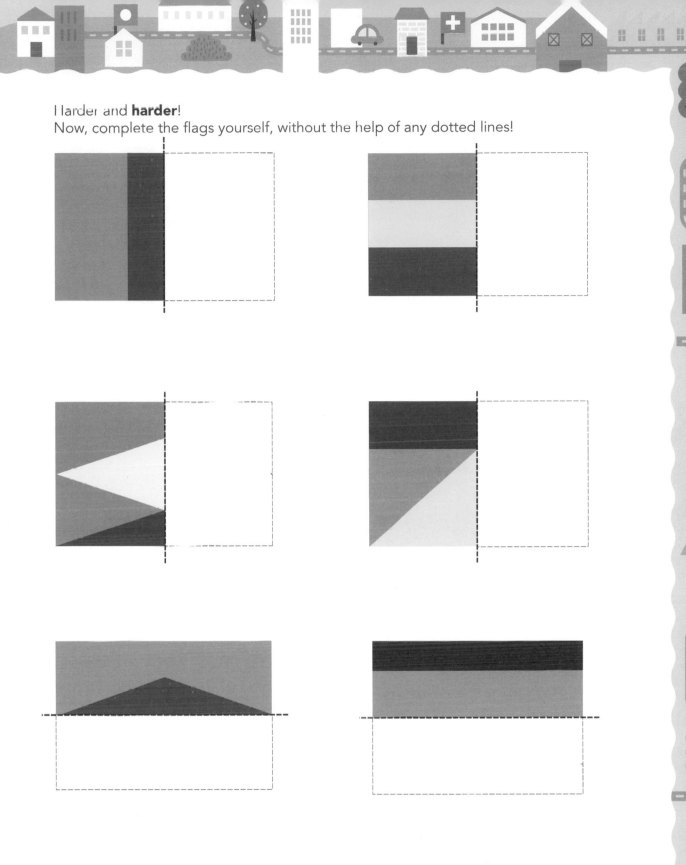

Time to Choose

Gea and I have to find the symmetrical flags among those below. Can you help us?

Take a good look at all the flags and then use the stickers to divide them into two groups. Note: a flag can be symmetrical horizontally or vertically!

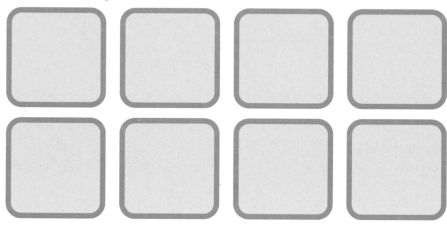

symmetrical flags

asymmetrical flags

Pay Attention to Details

Flags identify a place, so they must all be different from each other!
Sometimes it takes just one **detail** to make a flag distinctive. It's often the colors that make the difference, while sometimes it's how the colors are **arranged**.

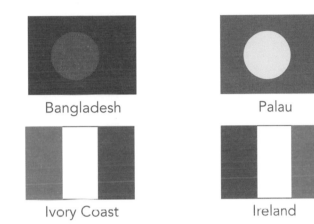

Bangladesh

Palau

Ivory Coast

Ireland

Now it's your turn! Look at the two groups of flags below: **they can be matched into pairs that look alike**, but there is **something** that makes them **different**. Connect the similar flags, then look at what makes them different.

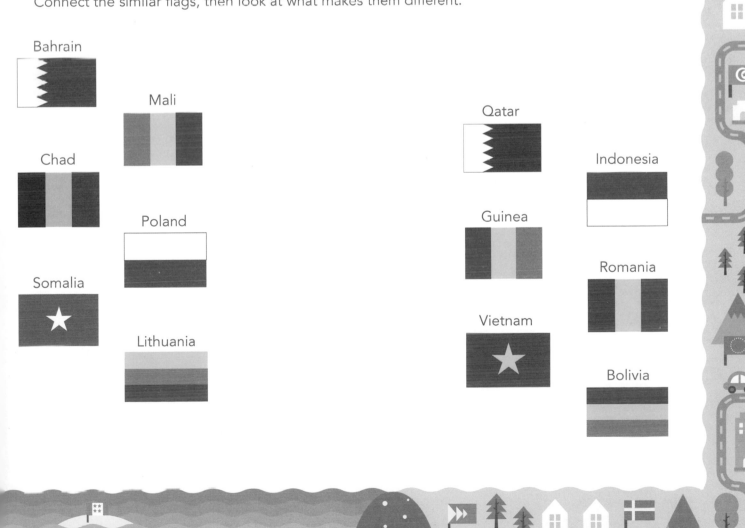

Bahrain

Mali

Qatar

Chad

Indonesia

Poland

Guinea

Somalia

Romania

Lithuania

Vietnam

Bolivia

Flag Sudoku

I love Sudoku.

Would you like to play? You have to fill the grid so that each row and each column contains 4 different flags. The rule is that **no rows, no columns, and no boxes can contain the same flag twice**, as shown in the example below.

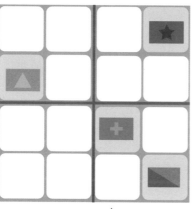

example

solution

Now, use the **stickers** to complete the grid.
But watch out: pay attention to details, and make sure that all the flags in the rows are different!

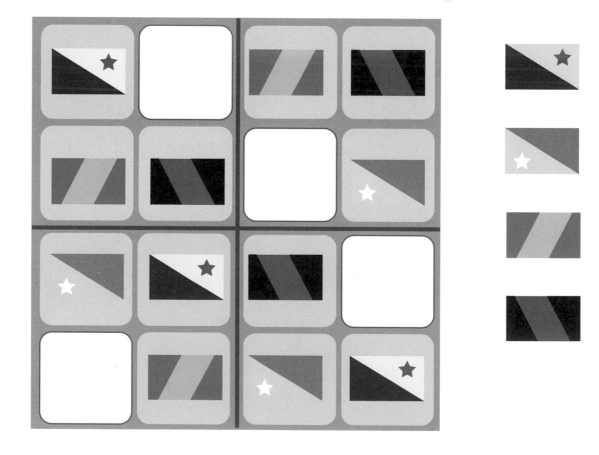

Harder and **harder**!

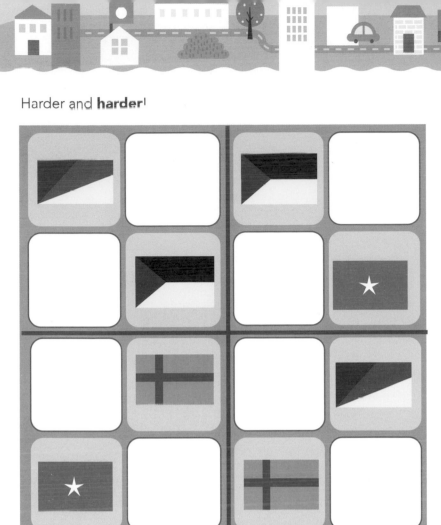

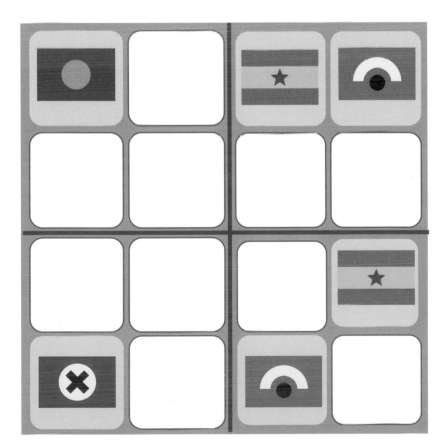

Flag Families

Some flags are very similar.

Although flags must be different from each other, they can be similar, highlighting **special bonds** between the countries they represent, such as speaking the same language or sharing the same culture or history. Basically, it's as if they were part of a big family!

To do this, you use similar colors or an identical symbol in a different color. A good example is the Scandinavian or **Nordic cross**, which is used to emphasize the link between the countries that use it.

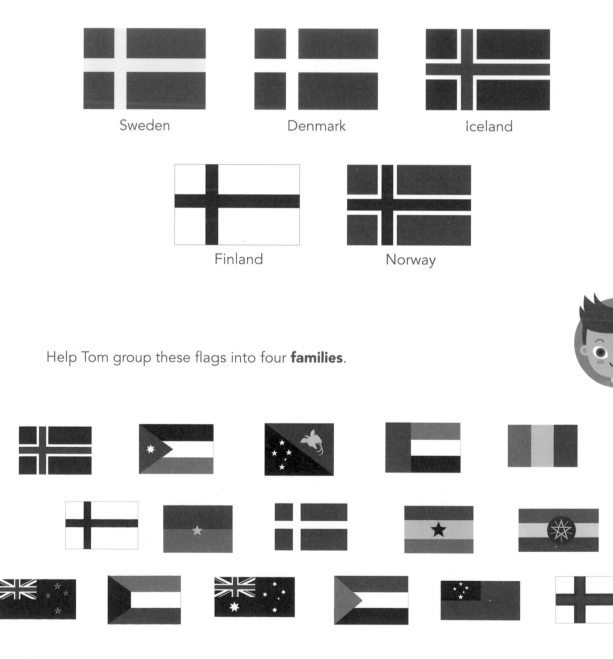

Sweden   Denmark   Iceland

Finland   Norway

Help Tom group these flags into four **families**.

Now, using the **stickers**, group the flags into the **four families** below.
Use the clue on the left to help you!

clue:

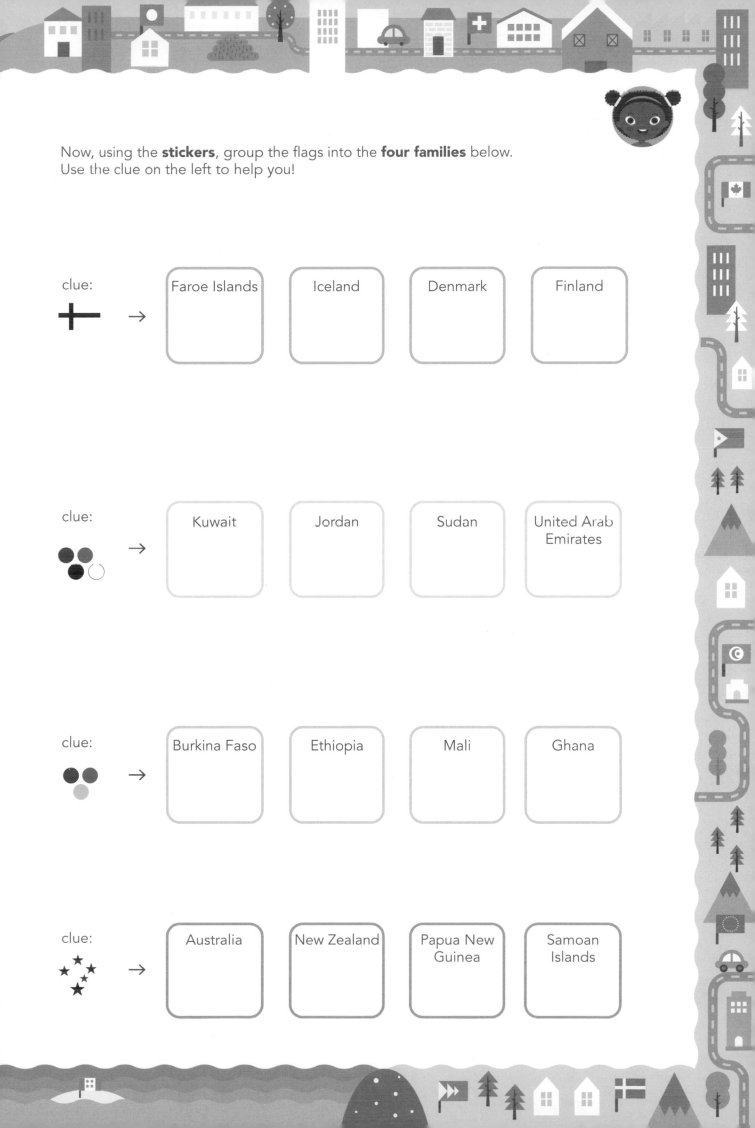

+ →

| Faroe Islands | Iceland | Denmark | Finland |

clue:

→

| Kuwait | Jordan | Sudan | United Arab Emirates |

clue:

→

| Burkina Faso | Ethiopia | Mali | Ghana |

clue:

→

| Australia | New Zealand | Papua New Guinea | Samoan Islands |

Let's Play with Pictures

A symbol can have many meanings. For example, it can indicate where a particular nation is located in the world.

A good example of this is the **Southern Cross**, a constellation that allows you to orient yourself in the **Southern Hemisphere**. The symbol of this constellation is used on some flags to indicate that those countries are located in this hemisphere.

Papua New Guinea

New Zealand

Australia

Samoan Islands

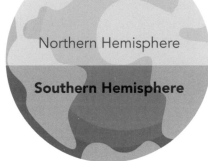

Northern Hemisphere

Southern Hemisphere

Use the stickers to help me complete these imaginary flag families.

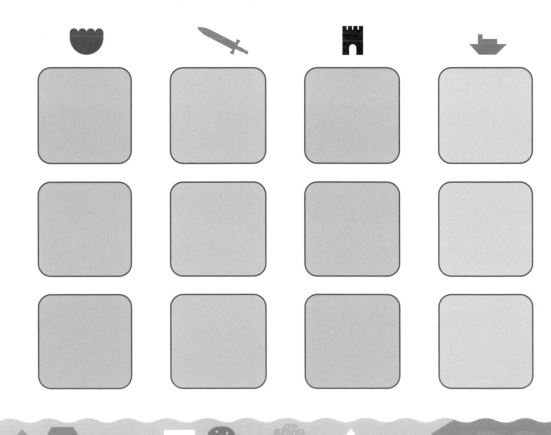

All Hands Ahoy!

I really like pirates.

Did you know they had **lots of different flags**? Check this out!

Tom, Gea, and I decided to play pirates. We made flags to show that we were on the same team.

Do you want to play with us? These are the flags we've designed.

Now, make your own, adding one small detail that makes it different from ours!
Use the **stickers** at the back of the book.

Color Families

Similar colors can be used to create a flag family.

There are sets of **colors** that indicate some countries are located in a certain area, for example, the "**Pan-African**" colors. Flags with these colors are designed to emphasize that the countries are on the African continent.

The colors are **red, gold,** and **green**:

or **black**, **red**, and **green**:

Burkina Faso   Ethiopia

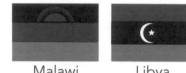

Malawi   Libya

Ghana

Kenya

Tom, Ben, and I belong to the Future Geographers Club, and its colors are **blue**, **green**, and **white**. We made our flags using the symbols that represent us.

Using the stickers, find the flags of our other friends who belong to our fantastic club. Make sure you only choose those with the **right colors**.

Let's Unite Flags

It's also possible to create a flag by uniting other flags.

This is done to highlight a particular link between countries, or to remember events in the country's history.

A good example is the **South African** flag, which is a combination of the flags of the **African National Congress**, the **United Kingdom**, and **Holland**.

These three flags represent the people of South Africa.

Let's create some **new flags** by uniting existing flags.
Find the **stickers** that combine the two flags.

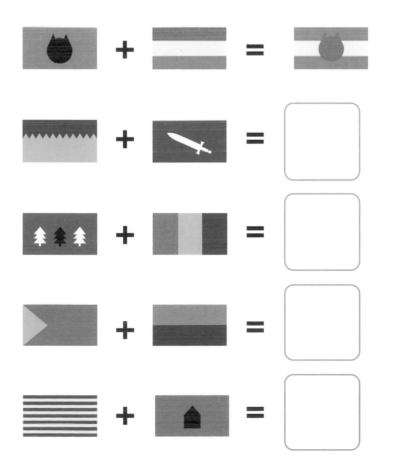

Follow the Rules

We've now looked at all the tips for creating a good flag.

The 5 principles are:
• keep it **simple**
• use meaningful **symbols**
• only use a **few colors**
• **no lettering**
• it must be **distinctive**, or indicate **links with other countries** or **its history**, using symbols or colors

Can you help me find the flags that follow the rules?

  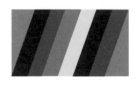

  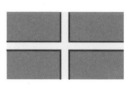

Now that you know all the principles for designing a flag, you should also know that there are some flags that don't follow the rules.

For example, the flag of Colorado has a large C, the flag of South Africa has lots of colors, and the flag of Nepal isn't a rectangle.

Nepal

Colorado

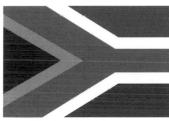

South Africa

I've decided to make a very special flag, without following any of the rules.
I want to design a flag with lots of colors, symbols, and lettering. You should design an **extravagant flag**, too, and then have fun coloring it!

Raise the Flag!

Did you know that there are rules for flying national flags? I only just found out!

• The flag must be raised at **sunrise** and lowered at **sunset**. It can only be displayed at night if it's **properly illuminated**.

• If the national flag is displayed alongside other flags, they must all be flown at the **same height**.

• If the national flag is flown alongside just one other flag, the latter must always be on the **left**.

• If, on the other hand, it's flown with two other flags, it must be in the **center**.

• If there are lots of flags, perhaps at an international event, they must be displayed in the **alphabetical order** of the country hosting the event, or the order of the **English alphabet**.

Circle the two pictures below that show common flag-flying mistakes.

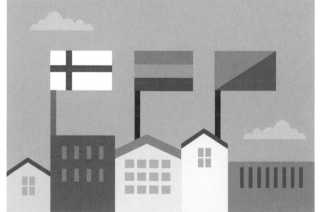

Shall We Play a Game?

Let's play a fun game that'll take us around the world. It's called the Goose Game.

We'll use the cards we made for the "Guess the Flag!" game as our tokens, and we'll roll our color die. On the next page, you'll find a world map, with lots of colored circles that represent the spaces on the board.

The rules of the game are very simple: the players take turns rolling the color die, then they move their flag to the next circle of the color they rolled.

Be careful though: on some circles you'll find instructions, and on others there's a ship or plane that will help you get around the board quicker.

The winner is the player who reaches the finish line first.

Last, but not least, **good luck**!

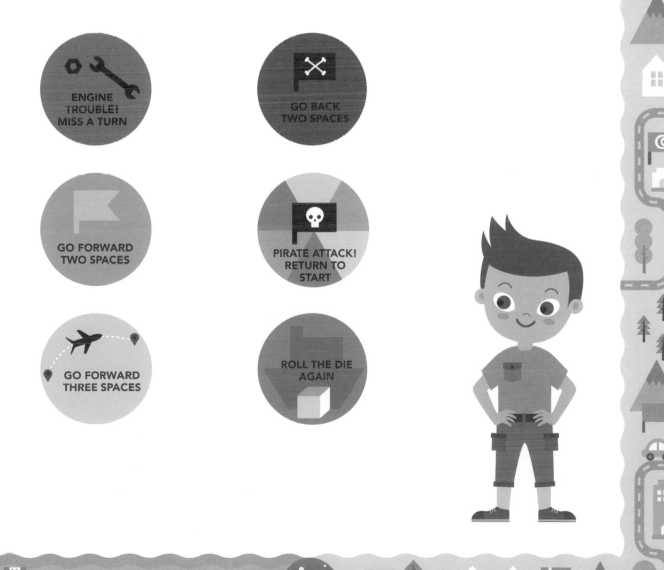

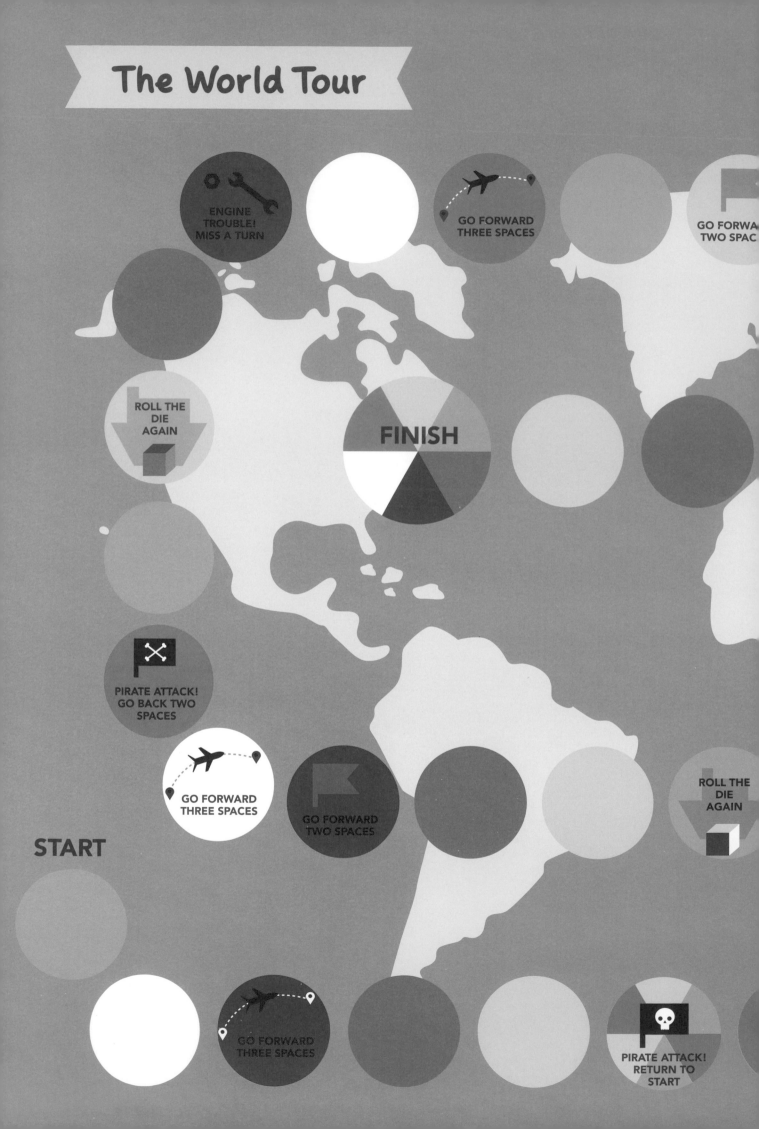

The Vexillologist Quiz

We now know a lot about how flags are made. See if you can answer the following questions. Use the book to help if you don't know the answer!

1. Vexillology is:
• a book of flags
• the study of flags

2. Is there such a thing as a **square** flag?
• Yes
• No

3. Flags must be **simple**:
• so that they look nice
• so that they are easy to remember and reproduce

4. Is there an **alphabet** made up of flags?
• Yes
• No

5. Flag families indicate:
• a link between the countries
• that they copied a flag because they liked it.

CONGRATULATIONS! YOU ARE NOW AN APPRENTICE VEXILLOLOGIST!

color your
rosette!

color your
rosette!

The Geographical Memory Game

There's nothing better than a game to help you remember everything you have learned! Let's make it together!

Stick the memory stickers at the back of the book onto a piece of cardboard. There are **16 pairs**, for a total of 32 cards.

Cut them out carefully, following the outlines.

Turn them over without looking at the pictures, and arrange them on a table or surface.

Play with a friend!

Take turns turning over two cards; if they're not the same, turn them back over.

If a player finds a pair of identical cards, they take them and continue to play until they stop finding pairs.

The game ends when there are no cards left. The winner is the person who collected the most pairs!

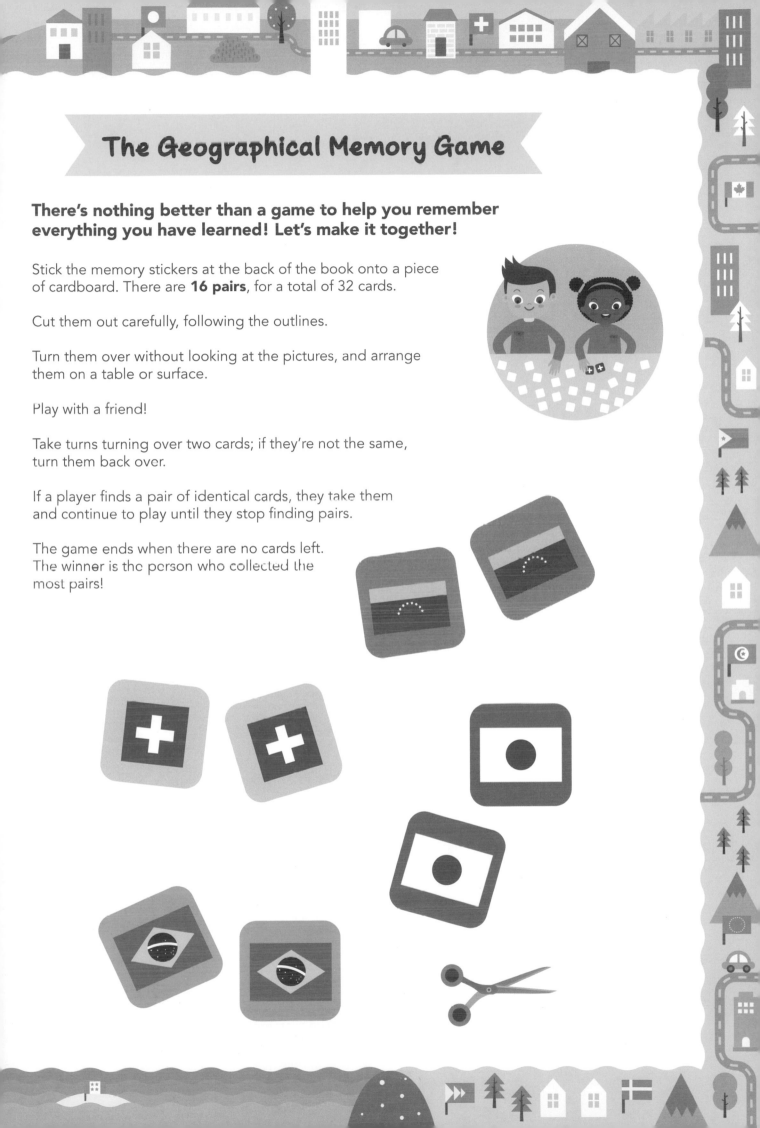

Answers

A Multitude of Flags! p. 6

Let's Study Flags p. 7
Answer: VEXILLOLOGY

What Are Flags Used For? p. 8

Just Flags? p. 9

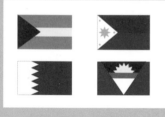

A Little Bit of History p. 10

The Oldest Flag in the World p. 11

What Is a Flag Composed Of? p. 12

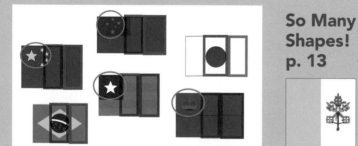

So Many Shapes! p. 13

A Flag Design Manual p. 14

1- A **GOOD** flag must be: simple — T
2- A **GOOD** flag must have: meaningful symbols — I
3- You **have** to use: a few colors — G
4- You **mustn't** use: lettering — E
5- A **GOOD** flag must be: different from all the others — R
Answer: TIGER

Simplicity p. 15

A Matter of Distance p. 16

Black and White p. 18

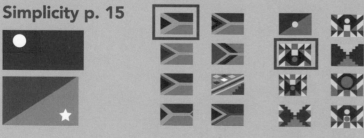
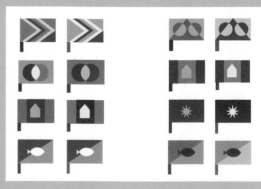

Hidden Meanings p. 20
Beastly Flags p. 21

A Flag Alphabet! p. 22

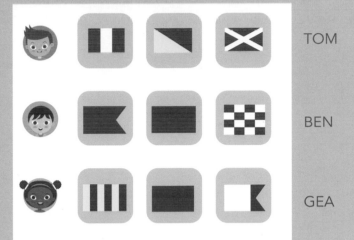

TOM

BEN

GEA

A Flag Alphabet! p. 23

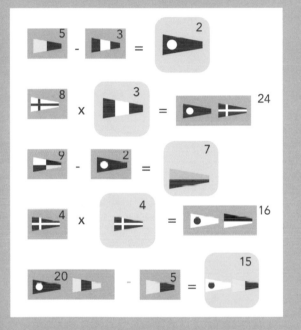

How Many Colors? p. 26

In which picture is the difference easier to spot? **The first one!**

same

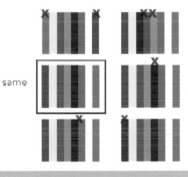

Get Out of the Maze p. 31

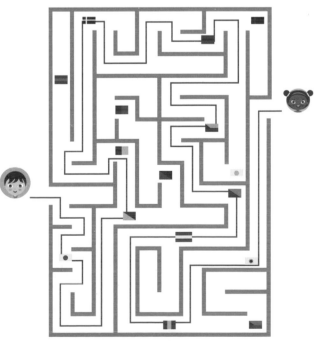

A Matter of Contrast p. 30

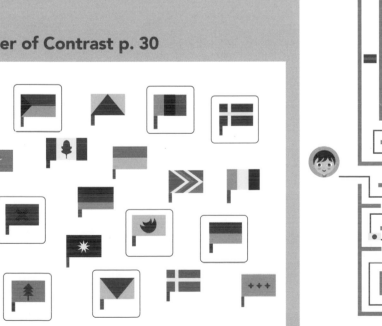

The Symmetry Game pp. 32-33

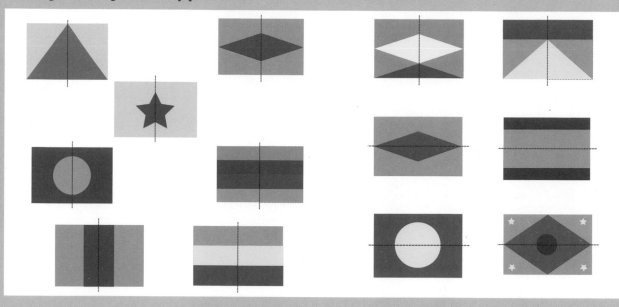

Time to Choose p. 34

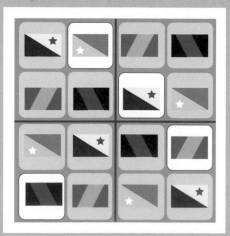

symmetrical flags:

asymmetrical flags:

Pay Attention to Details p. 35

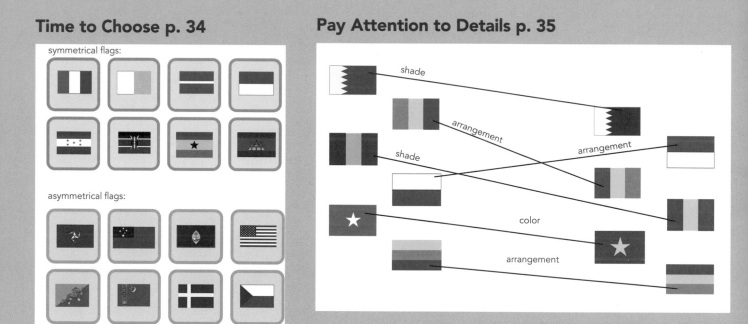

shade

shade

arrangement

arrangement

color

arrangement

Flag Sudoku p. 36

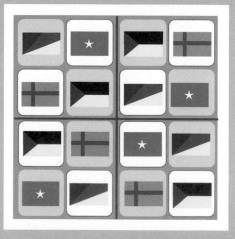

p. 37

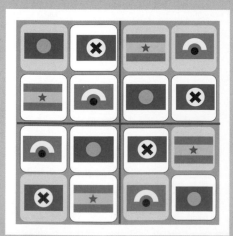

Flag Families pp. 38-39

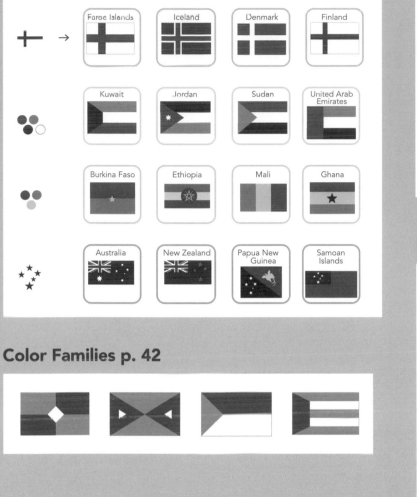

Color Families p. 42

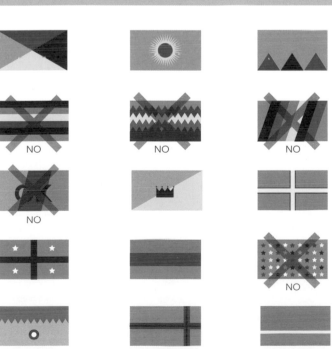

Follow the Rules p. 44

Let's Play with Pictures p. 40

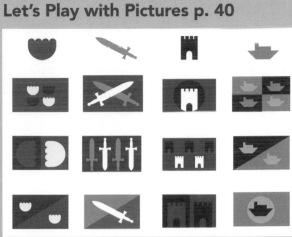

Let's Unite Flags p. 43

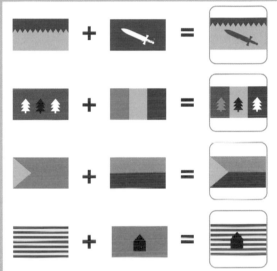

Raise the Flag p. 46

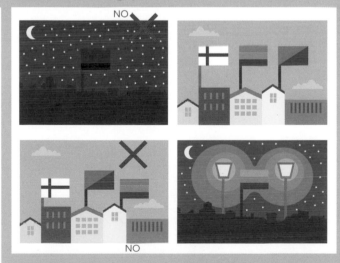

The Vexillologist Quiz p. 50

1. **Vexillology** is the study of flags
2. Is there such a thing as a square flag? **Yes**
3. Flags must be **simple** so that they are easy to remember and reproduce
4. Is there an **alphabet** made up of flags? **Yes**
5. **Flag families** indicate a link between the countries

Paola Misesti

Paola was born in Como in 1970 and has been living in Zurich with her family since 2011. She is an educator and teaches Italian to foreign students, and has also written and cowritten educational creativity and design books. She has been training educators, teachers, and parents for many years, and does workshops and educational projects in kindergartens and elementary schools. For the past 10 years, she has been sharing her experiences and materials online, on the homemademamma.com website.

Agnese Baruzzi

Agnese has a degree in graphic design from ISIA (Institute of Higher Education in the Artistic Industries) in Urbino. Since 2001, she has been working as an illustrator and author: she has created numerous children's books in both Italy and abroad. She holds workshops for children and adults, collaborating with schools and libraries.

White Star Kids™ is a trademark of White Star s.r.l.

© 2022 White Star s.r.l.
Piazzale Luigi Cadorna, 6
20123 Milan, Italy
www.whitestar.it

Originally published in 2022 as *Mad for Geography—Flags* by White Star, this North American version titled *All About Flags Awesome Activity Book* is published in 2023 by Fox Chapel Publishing Company, Inc. Reproduction of its contents is strictly prohibited without written permission from the rights holder.

Happy Fox Books is an imprint of Fox Chapel Publishing Company, Inc., 903 Square Street, Mount Joy, PA 17552.

ISBN 978-1-64124-332-2

To learn more about the other great books from Fox Chapel Publishing, or to find a retailer near you, call toll-free 800-457-9112 or visit us at *www.FoxChapelPublishing.com*.

We are always looking for talented authors.
To submit an idea, please send a brief inquiry to acquisitions@foxchapelpublishing.com.

Printed in China
First Printing

P. 6: A MULTITUDE OF FLAGS!

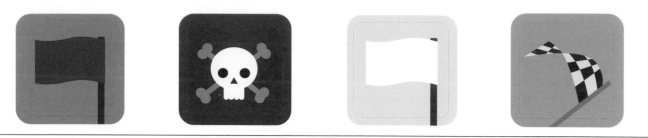

P. 10: A LITTLE BIT OF HISTORY

P. 11: THE OLDEST FLAG IN THE WORLD

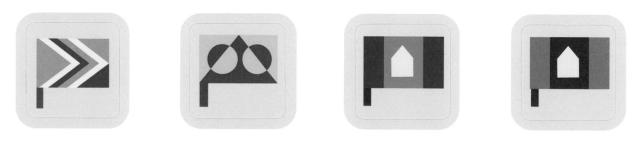

P. 18: BLACK AND WHITE

P. 20: HIDDEN MEANINGS

P. 21: BEASTLY FLAGS

P. 22: A FLAG ALPHABET!

  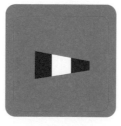 

P. 23: A FLAG ALPHABET! NUMBERS

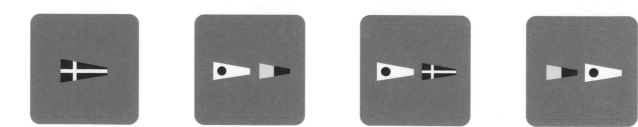

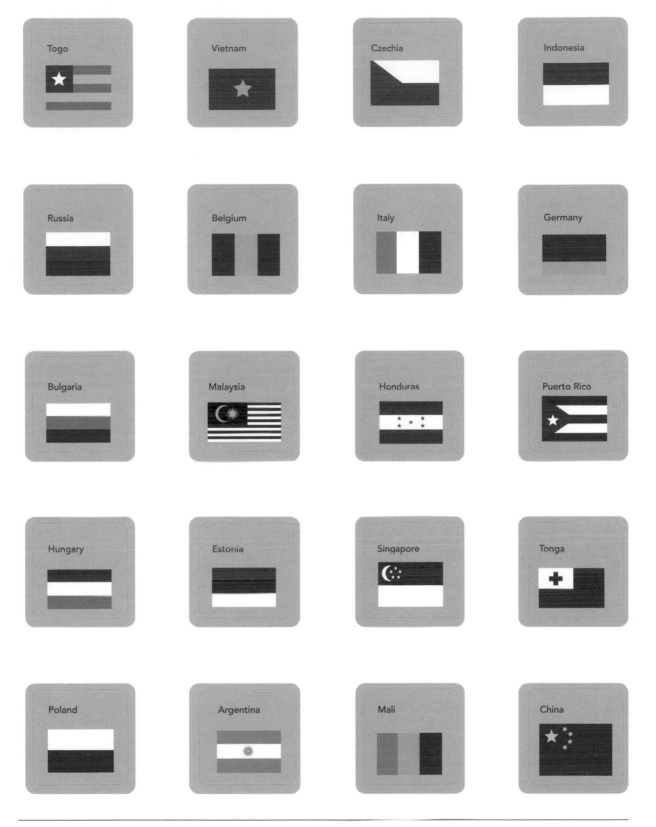

P. 30: A MATTER OF CONTRAST

P. 30: A MATTER OF CONTRAST

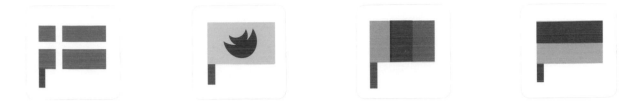

P. 34: TIME TO CHOOSE

P. 36: FLAG SUDOKU

P. 37: FLAG SUDOKU A

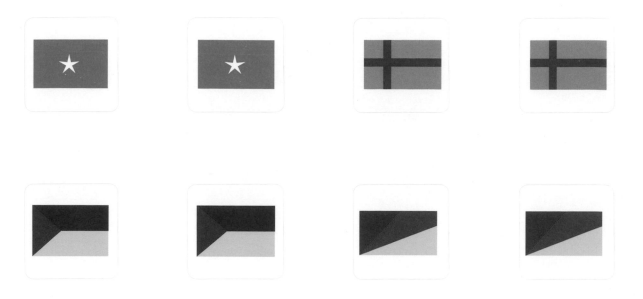

P. 37: FLAG SUDOKU B

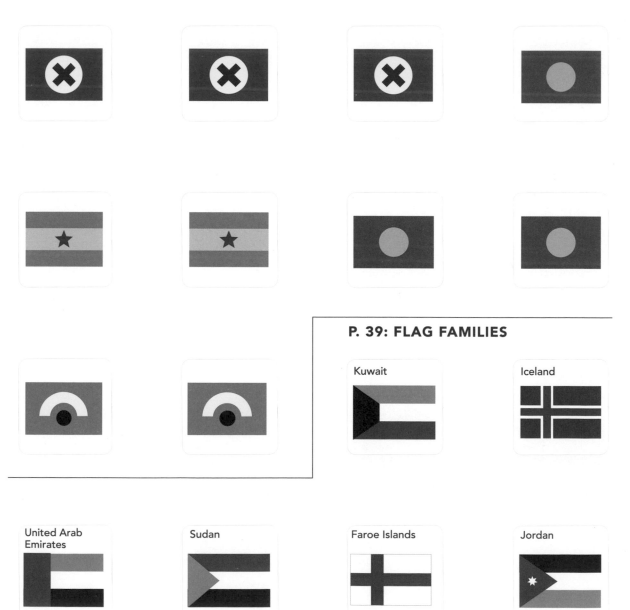

P. 39: FLAG FAMILIES

Kuwait

Iceland

United Arab
Emirates

Sudan

Faroe Islands

Jordan

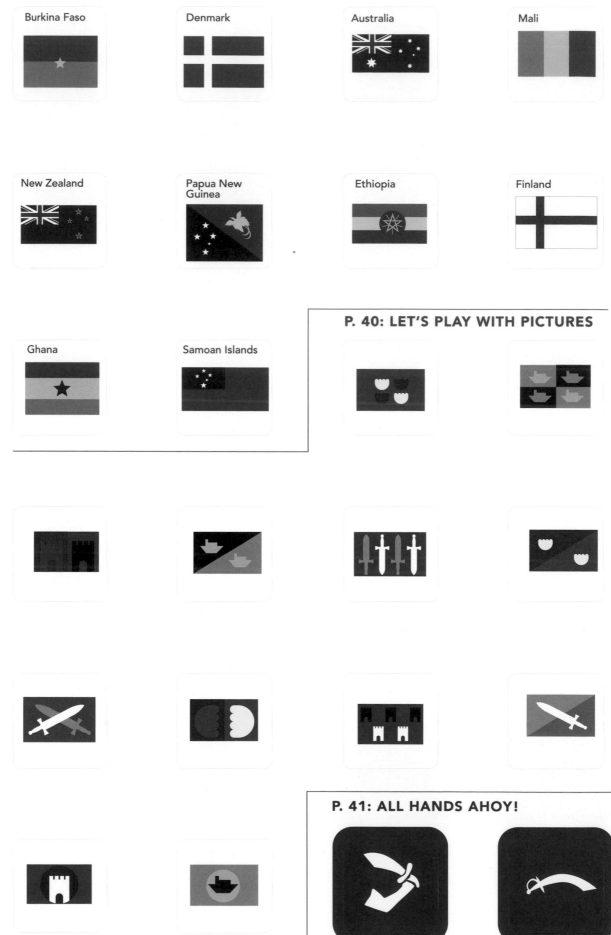

P. 39: FLAG FAMILIES

Burkina Faso

Denmark

Australia

Mali

New Zealand

Papua New Guinea

Ethiopia

Finland

Ghana

Samoan Islands

P. 40: LET'S PLAY WITH PICTURES

P. 41: ALL HANDS AHOY!

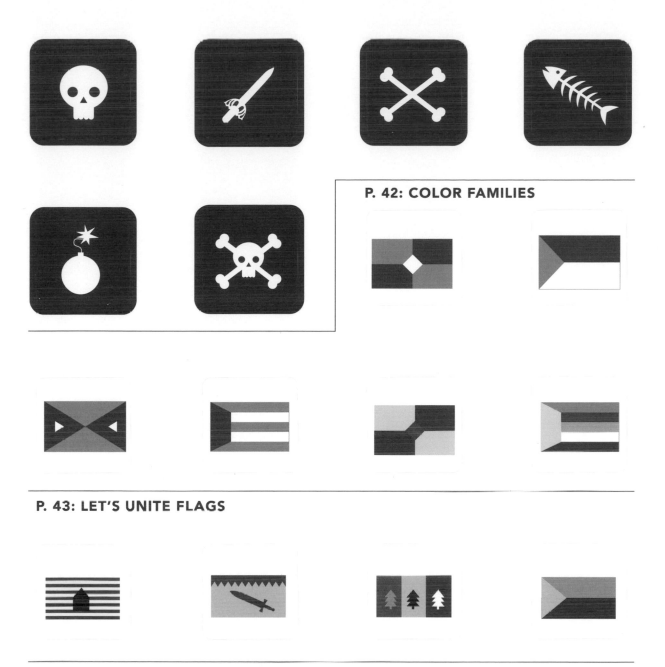

P. 42: COLOR FAMILIES

P. 43: LET'S UNITE FLAGS

P. 51: THE GEOGRAPHICAL MEMORY GAME

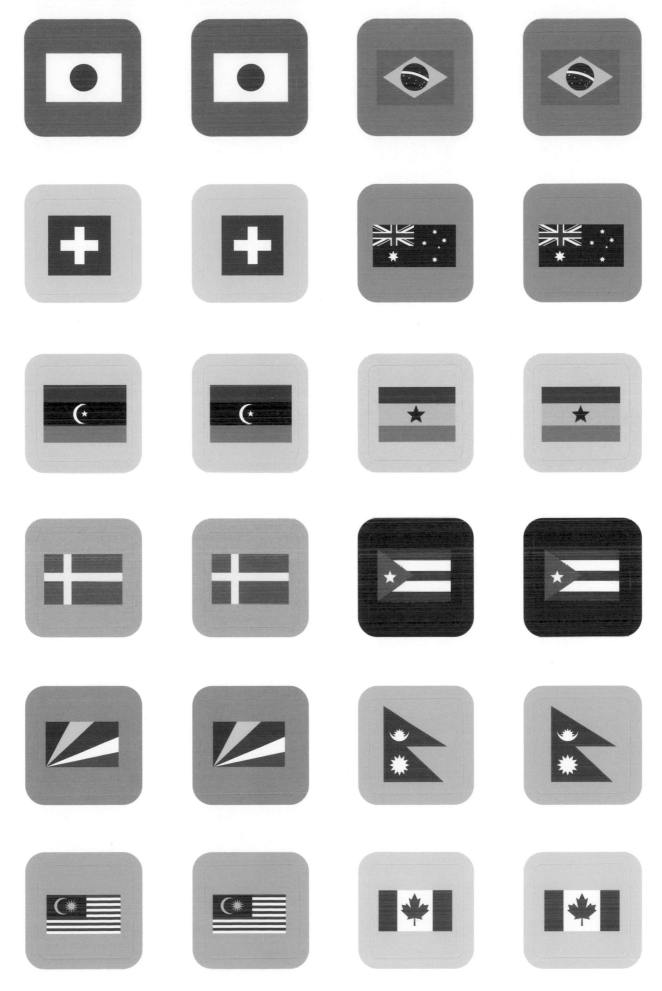